Creating and Consuming Media Messages with Purpose:

A Guide for Parents

Jennifer W. Shewmaker, Ph.D. and Amy Boone, M.Ed.

Gifted
EDUCATION

Edited by: Molly A. Isaacs-McLeod, JD, LL.M.
Interior design: The Printed Page
Cover design: Kelly Crimi

Published by
Gifted Unlimited, LLC
12340 U.S. Highway 42, No. 453
Goshen, KY 40026
www.giftedunlimitedllc.com

ISBN: 978-1-953360-24-3

Printed and bound in the United States of America using partially recycled paper.

Acknowledgments

We would like to thank Abilene Christian University and David Lipscomb University for creating space to explore ideas and learn in community. We are grateful for our colleagues as they regularly join us in our adventures in learning. Thank you to Dr. Mary Christopher for her leadership in the field of Gifted Education. We would also like to thank our families for their support and their belief in the importance of our pursuits.

Contents

Introduction

Child and adolescent development

Teens and tweens spend hours on electronic devices, including TVs, Smartphones, computers and tablets. They are inundated with media messages from many sources—company advertisements, social influencers, news reports, TV programs, movies and others. But they do not yet have the ability to understand the difference between advertisements, entertainment, and opinion.

Still, the images and narratives they absorb from media shape the way that they see the world—and themselves. Our job as adults is to help empower children to be active media consumers and creators.

The bioecological model

All forms of media have been identified as important socializing forces that deliver messages to children and adolescents about identity (ter Bogt, Engels, Bogers, 2010).

The bioecological model is a useful way to understand the effects of media on our children's development. It can help explain how environmental factors can affect a developing person's response to media messages.

The bioecological model, developed by Urie Bronfenbrenner (1979; 1992, 2005; Bronfenbrenner & Morris, 1998; 2006), says that both a person's temperament and the setting in which she lives lead one to learn, think, and grow in particular ways.

Bronfenbrenner says that a developing person's setting is made up of several interacting systems. These include the microsystem, which is made up of those closest to and most involved with the individual, such as the family, friends, school, and close community.

The exosystem is made up of those systems that are further removed but with which the person or those in their microsystem, such as parents, tend to interact regularly. This includes media, the parent's work environment, and other factors.

Lastly, the macrosystem is the larger system in which the individual functions, and includes things like the culture, federal laws and systems.

There are four components within this model that are important to understand in light of child and adolescent development. These are:

- Process
- Person
- Context
- Time

(PPCT; Bronfenbrenner, 2005, Bronfenbrenner & Morris, 2006)

To understand child development, we need to consider each of these four components. For example, each individual develops through the **process** of interacting with those within their immediate environment. This includes close relationships, such as family and peers.

A person's development is also influenced through interactions that she has with things within the wider (or macro) environment, such as media and marketing. At the same time, it is important for us to understand that elements of the **person** her- or himself, such as temperament and past experience, will influence the individual's interpretations, experiences of and responses to their interactions with these different systems. The **context** of the systems of influence (micro, exo and macro) shapes the child's understanding of and ability to respond to interactions with media and marketing. The **time** in which he is growing and learning influences the type of environment that the child will engage with as they develop (Shewmaker, 2015).

Critique and challenge the messages

Bronfenbrenner viewed the process of development as one in which the child can learn to fit into the existing environment and expectations, but also can change the order of things through their own actions (Tudge, Mokrova, Hatfield, & Karnik, 2009). When we provide children with the tools to critique and challenge the messages from media and marketing, they can become change makers. Their actions through media literacy programs, activism, and creation can lead to change in their environment.

Adolescents are in the process of constructing their identity, and the media is one of the influences in their lives that they use to help them figure out who they are, who they want to be, and who they think they should be. Adolescents are active media users, making sense of what they see and hear from their own individual perspective and experience.

Developmental research has clearly demonstrated that until age 8, children cannot separate persuasive messages from entertainment. Even pre-teens and those in their early teens are at a disadvantage in identifying advertisements when they are presented online rather than on television or in print (An, Jin, & Park, 2014; Rozendaal, Buijzen, & Valkenburg, 2011; Soontae & Stern, 2011; Mallinckrodt & Mizerski, 2007; Gunter, Oates & Blades, 2005; Oates, Blades, & Gunter, 2002). These facts make it more important than ever for adults to pay attention to the media that children and adolescents consume and to consider how our children can become active, critical media consumers.

Children and media use

Research shows that children spend an average of 5 hours on electronic devices per day (Crouch, 2016). Recent research has noted that 42% of children ages 0-8 now have their own tablet and 98% of children aged 0-18 years live in a home with a television and a mobile device. Additionally, 47% of tweens and 57% of teens reported having a television in their room. And 42% of children aged 0 to 8, 34%

aged 8 to 12 and 37% aged 13-18 live in houses where the TV is on "always" or "most of the time." Total screen media time each day for children aged 0-8 was reported as 2 hours and 19 minutes. Children ages 8-12 reported being exposed to media an average of 5:55 hours a day and 13–18-year-olds reported media usage at 8:56 hours each day (Rideout, 2015; 2017). When we consider entertainment screen media, 8–12-year-olds spend an average of 4:44 hours a day while teens spend 7:22, not including time spent for school or homework (Rideout & Robb, 2019).

Videos and more videos

The biggest change in recent years has been the increase in video viewing, with the number of young people reporting that they watch videos, such as those on YouTube and TikTok, everyday doubling since 2015. Adolescents also report that the time they spend watching videos has doubled since 2015, increasing from half an hour to an hour per day (Rideout & Robb, 2019).

The development of mobile technology means increased accessibility, which makes media messages even more powerful. This exposure is a key issue when considering the way that children use media today. Mobile devices that access media, such as the iPhone, Android, and iPad, have made media readily accessible to an ever-increasing number of young people. Ownership of mobile devices among 8–18-year-olds has increased dramatically over the past five years. Of children surveyed, 98% said they have mobile devices in their homes—45% of children, 77% of tweens and 100% of teens have their own mobile device, either a tablet or a smartphone.

Smartphones and social media

Smartphones have morphed from a vehicle for communication to a way to connect with media. Young people who own a cell phone tend to use it more often to play or watch media than they do for talking to another person (Rideout, 2015; 2017). Interestingly, in recent years we have seen an increase in the use of mobile devices to connect with others via social media. Some 58% of teens use social media, spending an average of two hours each day on it. This tends to be an activity that increases with age, with only 15% of 8–12-year-olds reporting the regular use of social media while 58% of teens report its use (Rideout & Robb, 2019; Rideout, 2015).

Supporting social media development

As with all developmental skills, caregivers need to play an active role as their child learns to use media, particularly social media. Social media use is made up of five key behaviors (Meshi et al., 2015). People use social media in order to (1) broadcast information; (2) receive feedback on this information; (3) observe the broadcasts of others; (4) provide feedback on the broadcasts of others; and (5) compare themselves with others.

It is helpful to think about how social media works and how it has evolved by using Bronfenbrenner's Bioecological Model. Social media provides users with a consistent supply of social rewards. Likes, friend requests, comments on a post or positive responses to a post activate our brain's reward system and shapes reinforcement learning. Face-to-face social interactions activate the reward system in the same way. Social media platforms have evolved to provide more interaction and more social rewards, which is what makes them so attractive.

When you think about how to guide your child in learning to use social media effectively, think of it in the same way that you have helped them learn how to do other things, such as tying their shoes, riding a bike, roller skating and so forth. When your child began to do these things, they were just learning, so you were right alongside them, talking with them about how to do it and watching and correcting them as they did the activity. Guiding your child to use social media effectively can be done in the same way. That means, when your child first starts using social media, you should talk with them about it first, let them know the challenges that social media can present, such as taking up time you might be doing other things, providing opportunities for communicating with people you don't know who may be dishonest or intend harm, and even the way that when communicating with someone when we're not face to face, we may not pick up on cues like body language, facial expression, and voice tone and end up hurting each other's feelings or misunderstanding one another.

Once you've discussed the use of social media with your child and the things to look out for to help them be effective communicators in that medium, you can then help them set up their own social media profile if you feel comfortable doing so. We tend to recommend that children not do this until middle school at the earliest and even then, that they only use platforms that allow for easy blocking of people whom they don't know. When you do feel that your child is ready to have their own profile, it is important that in the beginning they understand that you will be monitoring their use of social media in order to help them use it effectively. That means that you will see who is messaging them and who they are messaging, and you can see what they are posting. This allows for specific conversations about any issues that may arise. For example, if your child has an Instagram account, their profile can be set to private, so they have to give permission for other accounts to follow them or contact them. You can walk through looking at who may be requesting to connect or message them and talk about why they should or should not give that person access to communicating with them.

You might also use this time of skill building to help your child navigate miscommunications that may arise. For example, if they seem to be getting into an argument with someone on social media, you can stop and talk with them about it. Ask them if this is someone they know or don't know in face-to-face life. Then follow up with questions to help them think through if their communications may have been misinterpreted or if they may be misinterpreting the other person. You can ask them, "If you were talking with this person face to face, how would you talk with them? What would you say? What questions would you ask?" The goal is to help your child build their skills in online communication, building upon the skills they have learned to use in face-to-face communications.

Media messages can be positive or negative

The increase in media exposure and use of media to share about one's self has made it vitally important for those living and working with children and adolescents to understand how media affects their development and to identify strategies that can create critical, empowered media consumers and makers. It's important for us to remember that media is a tool that can be used to promote both positive and negative messages to our children and allow our children to share their own perspectives through media creation. While some media can lead to negative outcomes, media messages that challenge stereotypes and promote complex views of people can open avenues for great conversations.

This book has been created to help parents and caregivers provide opportunities for their children to begin to create and consume media messages with purpose, empowering them to be active consumers and creators. You can find a deeper look into the research and an extension of the themes discussed in this book, with a focus on sexualized media, in the book *Sexualized media messages and our children: Teaching kids to be smart critics and consumers* by Dr. Jennifer W. Shewmaker.

Media Intent and Audience

Question: How can parents help their children, teens and tweens understand the intent of a piece of media and what audience that media is targeting?

Overview: This content will focus on media's intent and audience. When a person encounters a media message, they must ask where the message originated. They should also consider who is the target audience of the media message. The conversation starter and activity for this session include identifying types of language used in media messages and how a media message captures the attention of the consumer.

What does the research say?

We want to investigate how children can become empowered to critique media, with a focus on helping them identify the intent of the media creator and the intended audience. What is media, after all, but the creation of something that shares an individual or group's worldview with others? When children begin to understand that each piece of media or marketing that they consume has been crafted to promote a particular perspective, they can learn to identify that perspective and ask themselves how they feel about it. Parents can help by giving children the ability to do three things:

1. Become aware of what they are consuming,
2. Identify the worldview being presented, and
3. Decide what they think of it.

It is good to be critically aware of the meanings and implications of the media and platforms with which we interact. The recognition that a piece of media may be sending messages that do not align with one's core values is the first step to becoming a critical media consumer. Some of these strategies have been adapted from ideas presented in the work of Renee Hobbs (2011), a media literacy expert. Her book *Digital and Media Literacy: Connecting Culture and Classroom* provides an excellent guide to understanding the importance of digital and media literacy along with information and specific plans for using literacy activities in the classroom with varied curriculum.

Steps to understanding intent and audience

First, ask a few questions about the target audience:

- ❍ Who does this message come from?
- ❍ Who is the target audience according to the developer?
- ❍ Paying attention to what you see and hear, who seems to be the target audience to you?

Next, we want to help our children consider the messages that are being shared. As we explore this issue, we can ask questions such as:

- ❍ What message is clearly displayed through words, music, images, and stories?
- ❍ What about the unspoken messages?
- ❍ Are there impressions that you get very clearly whether they are or are not spoken?

Last, we will help children consider the values that are being shared in media messages. It's important that children know that each piece of media that they consume represents some sort of value, and to learn to ask themselves what those values are, how they compare to the child's own value system, and how they feel about those being represented through that piece of media. We'll guide our children through considering this by asking them to consider,

- What values are presented?
- What positive and negative messages come through?
- How do these compare to your own value system?

Renee Hobbs. *Digital and Media Literacy: Connecting Culture and Classroom.* (Thousand Oaks, California: Corwin Press, 2011). 232.

Conversation starter

Teens and tweens don't often think about the fact that media makers have intentions when they share their products and/or content. For example, over 50 years ago, the original Sesame Street team created a show targeted at young children to convey the value of community. The intention of the Sesame Street creators is quite overt, but often media creators target individuals and groups without being so obvious. This makes identifying the intentions of the media creator challenging, but you can help them begin to think about this more intentionally. Here are some ideas to help you start conversations with your child.

Let's get started!

- ❍ With your adolescent, brainstorm a list of several media sources they and you read/visit regularly. These might include local/regional/state/national news sources in print or television, social media sites, etc.
- ❍ Take a look at several of the sources to see what stories are trending and select a story that interests you and your child.
- ❍ Now look for your chosen story in each of the media sources you identified. As you read and observe, pay close attention! Identify what kind of language is used? Is it formal? Highly educated? Casual? Does it try to lure you into reading? How?
- ❍ Do different sources tell the story differently, maybe drawing different conclusions? How is it different?
- ❍ Lead your child in making conclusions about what various media sources are appealing to and who their audiences might be. Also, discuss with them how they can determine what to expect when turning to the various news sources for important information and why this is important.

Take it to the next level!

Your child is now more aware of various media sources and have identified their intent/audience. Now it's time to practice on an unsuspecting friend or adult! Think of a current newsworthy person or current event that various media outlets might represent differently based on their intent or audience. Using the prior knowledge from the activity above, create a news piece (print, audio, or video) from one specific perspective about this person or situation. Encourage your adolescent to consider the title/headline, word choice, emphasis, tone, and their audience's education level/expectation. After the news piece is complete, share it with the chosen friend/adult. Ask the viewer generic questions about the piece. What did they notice? What jumped out at them? What do they find appealing about the piece? Ask the friend if they think about WHO a media message is for and what that message might be. Then reveal why media intent matters when we are listening, watching, and processing various sources of information.

References

An, S., Jin, H. S., & Park, E. H. (2014). Children's Advertising Literacy for Advergames: Perception of the Game as Advertising. *Journal Of Advertising, 43*(1), 63-72. doi:10.1080/00913367.2013.795123

Bogt, T. t., Engels, R., Bogers, S., & Kloosterman, M. (2010). 'Shake It Baby, Shake It': Media Preferences, Sexual Attitudes and Gender Stereotypes Among Adolescents. *Sex Roles, 63*(11-12), 844-859. doi:10.1007/s11199-010-9815-1

Bronfenbrenner, U. (1979). *The Ecology of Human Development* (Cambridge, MA: Harvard University Press, 1979)

Bronfenbrenner, U. (1992). *Six Theories of Child Development: Revised Formulations and Current Issues*, ed. Ross Vasta (London: Jessica Kingsley) 187-249.

Bronfenbrenner, U. (2005). *Making Human Beings Human* (Thousand Oaks, CA: Sage).

Bronfenbrenner, U. & Morris, P. A. (1998). "The Ecology of Developmental Processes," in *Theoretical Models of Human Development*, ed. Richard M. Lerner, vol. 1 of *Handbook of Child Psychology*, 5th ed., ed. William Damon (New York: Wiley, 1998), 993-1028;

Bronfenbrenner, U. & Morris, P. A. (2006). "The Bioecological Model of Human Development," in *Theoretical Models of Human Development*, ed. Richard M. Lerner, vol. 1 of *Handbook of Child Psychology*, 5th ed., ed. William Damon (New York: Wiley).

Crouch, A. (2017). *The tech-wise family: everyday steps for putting technology in its proper place.* Grand Rapids : Baker Books, [2017].

Gunter, B., Oates, C., & Blades, M. (2005). *Advertising to Children on TV: Content, Impact, and Regulation.* Mahwah, N.J.: Routledge.

Mallinckrodt, V., & Mizerski, D. (2007). The effects of playing an advergame on young children's perceptions, preferences, and requests. *Journal of Advertising, 36*(2), 87-100.

Meshi, Tamir, and Heekeren, Trends in Cognitive Sciences, 2015. DOI 10.1016/j.tics.2015.09.004

Oates, C., Blades, M., & Gunter, B. (2002). Children and television advertising: When do they understand persuasive intent? *Journal Of Consumer Behaviour, 1*(3), 238.

Rideout, V., and Robb, M. B. (2019). *The Common Sense census: Media use by tweens and teens, 2019.* San Francisco, CA: Common Sense Media.

Rideout, V. (2017). The Common Sense census: Media use by kids age zero to eight. San Francisco, CA: Common Sense Media.

Rideout, V. (2015). The Common Sense census: Media use by tweens and teens. San Francisco, CA: Common Sense Media.

Rozendaal, E., Buijzen, M. and Valkenburg, P. (2011), "Children's understanding of advertiser's persuasive tactics," *International Journal of Advertising,* 30 (2), 329–50.

Shewmaker, J. W. (2015). Sexualized media messages and out children: Teaching kids to be smart critics and consumers. Santa Barbara, CA: Praeger.

Soontae, A., & Stern, S. (2011). Mitigating the effects of advergames on children. *Journal Of Advertising, 40*(1), 43-56.

Tudge, J. H., Mokrova, I., Hatfield, B. E., & Karnik, R. B. (2009). Uses and misuses of Bronfenbrenner's bioecological theory of human development. *Journal Of Family Theory & Review, 1*(4), 198-210. doi:10.1111/j.1756-2589.2009.00026.x

Identity

Question: How can parents help children explore connections between identity online and in face-to-face life?

Overview: This section will focus on identity. In their study of interaction with media, children will explore connections between identity in real life and identity online. Children will have the opportunity to consider how they and others use social media to represent themselves. Together, parents and child will explore the idea that identity online is chosen and curated, with different degrees of connection to face-to-face identity.

What does the research say about identity and social media?

Children and adolescents are in the process of constructing their identity, and media is one of the influences in their lives that guides them in that process. It's been suggested that media influence development in adolescents in areas such as building social connections as well as forming identity (Twenge, Martin & Spitzberg, 2019). Research has found that adolescents report increasing use of social media (Twenge et al. 2019, Rideout & Robb, 2019). In a 2018 national survey, 81% of teenagers reported using social media, with 70% of those teens reporting that they use it more than once a day, 38% saying they use it multiple times an hour and 16% "almost constantly" (Rideout & Robb, 2018). More recent surveys have shown that teens continue to spend about 1 hour 10 minutes per day on social media, but more are reporting using it every day, up to 63% in 2019 from 45% in 2015 (Rideout & Robb, 2019).

The availability of mobile devices with cameras and the increase in the existence and use of social media platforms means that young people now have the ability to express themselves and shape the sharing and representation of their identity in ways that are unprecedented (Tshidzumba, 2019; Lin et al, 2015). Research suggests that impression management is something that users consider when on social media, and many choose to represent their "ideal self," which is the representation of traits and attributes that a person would like to possess or believes someone else would like them to have instead of their "actual self," or the representation of the traits or attributes that a person believes they actually have (Higgins, 1987; Siibak, 2009).

Adolescents tend to join social media networks for social reasons and use their visual self-presentation in strategic ways. They often choose to share images that represent their ideal self, based on their understanding of what they perceive as being important to others with high social standing either online or both online and offline, and an adolescent may choose to represent themselves in different ways depending on the online peer group that they are trying to connect with socially (Siibak, 2009).

When using social media, people may work to extend their offline persona, but they may also choose to use the medium to create a new persona, reinventing themselves through the platform (Popescu, 2019).

It's also important to know that social media can impact the social experiences of teens by offering new opportunities for compensatory behaviors that would be less likely in face-to-face interactions (Nesi, Choukas-Bradley & Prinstein, 2018). Research on the effects of computer mediated communication, which includes social media interactions, supports the concept of "online disinhibition effect" (Suler, 2004). The online disinhibition effect means that specific features of the online environment, such as not receiving immediate feedback from peers due to the asynchronous nature of the communication and not being able to pick up on verbal or facial cues of others, create a setting in which people are more likely to do or say things that would not in a face-to-face context. For example, one time when I was working with a group of adolescents, two of them got into a back and forth on social media that almost came to a physical altercation the next time we were together in person. When we had the chance to talk in person about what had happened, it turned out that the two of them had very different ideas about the friendliness of the exchange. One person thought that they were good-naturedly joking around with one another, while the other person felt that they had been personally insulted and demeaned. Because these two were not having this exchange in person, neither could use the social cues of voice tone, facial expression, or body language to note the other person's response. The one who thought they were being funny would most likely have regulated their behavior differently if they had been able to pick up on those cues from their friend, but in a social media environment that is not possible.

Remember, media is a tool. It can be used to build social connections and share oneself in constructive ways, and it can also be used to construct a representation of identity that may not be accurate. It's our goal to help children identify their own reasons for using social media, consider how they want others to perceive them and think about how their use of these platforms contributes to their desired presentation or takes away from it.

Conversation starter

We recognize that social media threads are filled with keyboard warriors who feel safely emboldened behind their screen. Many people react and chat online in ways they would never engage in person. Behind the screen, many feel a false sense of safety. Commenters will confront and challenge others in caustic and disrespectful ways which are also different from how they would behave face to face. These online behaviors begin creating a second identity for an individual. A person may act and speak one way in person, but their online persona sounds like a different person.

Let's get started!

- ❍ Select ahead of time a video to use in this conversation. Search YouTube for a video of a person who presents themself as a good singer, but who clearly is not a good singer. Check the worst American Idol auditions as a starting place.
- ❍ Ask your child to verbally list or jot down on scratch paper words and phrases that they think describe themselves. You will refer back to this list at the end of the activity (AT THIS POINT, DO NOT REVEAL THE ACTIVITY OR TOPIC FOR THE DAY).
- ❍ Then ask them to list or jot down words or phrases that someone else would use to describe them (they may be some of the same or different descriptions).
- ❍ Show your child the video. Try to remain emotionless so your child doesn't pick up on your bias or feelings about the singer.
- ❍ At this point, you are going to actually model bad behavior in order to expose inappropriate online interaction. Tell your child the two of you are going to pretend this singer's clip was a social media post and you are going to leave a witty comment. Encourage your child to be clever and don't hesitate to mock the singer if you know your child can handle that.

- Once you and your child write your clever response, invite your child into your own thinking and process. You will now verbalize how that comment does not really reflect how you would respond to this person if you were face to face with them. In your thinking aloud, model a spirit of remorse through your realization.
- Invite your child into this thinking process. Lead your child to wondering if you both might want to rewrite a comment that would align with how you would respond in real life that has more compassion and kindness. You can lead your child in a direction that doesn't lie (no need to tell a person their singing is good when it isn't!), but to offer encouragement. For example, if a person were to offer a comment to a bad singer who had put themselves in a public space for others to hear, an encouraging word might be, "That was brave of you to audition."
- Looking back on their descriptive list of themselves from the beginning of the activity, discuss with your child why it is important for one's online identity to align with their in-person identity.

Take it to the next level!

Expanding on the concept of online disinhibition, engage your child in the following activity. Choose one side of the room to represent "strongly agree" and the other side of the room to represent "strongly disagree." Explain that the imaginary line between the two walls represents a continuum between the two polarities. Use any of the following questions and instruct your child to stand on the imaginary line where they see themselves to be.

1. When having a conversation with someone face to face my response is often based on their reaction.
2. When having a conversation with someone face to face, I wait for the other person to complete their sentence before responding.

3. When having a conversation with someone face to face, I often say something that risks my physical or emotional safety.
4. When engaging with someone online, I spend a long time thinking about how I will respond before typing.
5. When engaging with someone online, I picture the other person's reaction as I reply.
6. When engaging with someone online, I often say something that would risk my physical safety if I were face to face with the person.
7. When engaging with someone online, I often say something that calls into question the other person's character.

After each statement is read and your child moves to their chosen spot on the "line," invite them to voice their thoughts about where they have chosen to stand. Return to the conversation about disinhibition and ask them why people may feel less inhibition online than in real life. Discuss what this means about one's identity if a person's online presence is very different from how they interact face to face. Help them create a personal statement about how they will interact online that matches who they want to be in real life.

References

Higgins, E. T. (1987). Self-discrepancy: A theory relating self and affect. Psychological Review, 94, 319-340.

Nesi, J., Choukas-Bradley, S., & Prinstein, M. J. (2018). Transformation of Adolescent Peer Relations in the Social Media Context: Part 2-Application to Peer Group Processes and Future Directions for Research. Clinical Child & Family Psychology Review, 21(3), 295–319. https://doi.org/10.1007/s10567-018-0262-9

Popescu, M. M. (2019). Personal Online Identity-Branding or Impression Management. Buletin Stiintific, 24(1), 67–75. https://doi.org/10.2478/bsaft-2019-0008

Qiu, L., Lu, J., Yang, S., Qu, W., & Zhu, T. (2015). What does your selfie say about you? *Computers in Human Behavior*, *52*, 443–449. https://doi.org/10.1016/j.chb.2015.06.032

Rideout, V., and Robb, M. B. (2019). *The Common Sense census: Media use by tweens and teens, 2019*. San Francisco, CA: Common Sense Media.

Rideout, V. & Robb, M.B. (2018). *Social media, social life: Teens reveal their experiences.* San Francisco, CA: Common Sense Media.

Siibak, A. (2009). Constructing the Self through the Photo selection - Visual Impression Management on Social Networking Websites. Cyberpsychology: Journal of Psychosocial Research on Cyberspace, 3(1), Article 1. Retrieved from https://cyberpsychology.eu/article/view/4218

Suler, J. (2004). The online disinhibition effect. CyberPsychology & Behavior, 7(3), 321–326. https ://doi.org/10.1089/10949 3104129129 5.

Tshidzumba, N. A. (2019). The Selfie Culture: Identity Creation and Status Conferral on Social Media. *Gender & Behaviour*, *17*(3), 13577–13584. Retrieved from http://search.ebscohost.com/login.aspx?direct=true&AuthType=sso&db=a9h&AN=139753108&site=eds-live&scope=site

Twenge, J. M., Martin, G. N., & Spitzberg, B. H. (2019). Trends in US Adolescents' media use, 1976–2016: The rise of digital media, the decline of TV, and the (near) demise of print. Psychology of Popular Media Culture, 8(4), 329–345. https://doi.org/10.1037/ppm0000203

Implicit Bias

Question: In their study of consequences of perspectives in media, children will consider the reality of subconscious bias based on perspective.

Overview: In this section we will think about perspective and how it shapes how we see the world around us. We will also explore the ways our implicit or unconscious biases shape our perspectives. These are automatic associations we make about specific groups of people that affect the way that we respond to them. We may even be unaware of holding these beliefs, because these biases are deeply ingrained in our ways of understanding the world (Applebaum, 2019). The activities for this session challenges children to consider how perspective and bias can completely change the way someone or something is perceived. We'll take it to the next level by moving deeper into implicit bias in order to make children more aware of the unconscious biases they may hold.

What does the research say about subconscious bias?

Differences come in many forms, as can commonalities, and we can belong to many different kinship groups. Kinship groups are groups of people that have something in common (Banaji & Greenwald, 2013). As we grow up, all of us begin to learn how to tell who is a part of our kinship groups and who isn't. This social understanding helps us build connection, but it can also cause us to feel disconnected and unable to relate to or have empathy for those who we perceive as different from ourselves. Noticing differences isn't bias, it's the automatic assumptions that we make about people due to those differences that are connected to bias.

As we learn how to relate to others who are similar to or different from us, we develop implicit or unconscious biases. Our biases may be positive or negative, and can focus around gender, race, weight, height, skin tone or any other aspect of a person's identity. Every person has implicit biases, or blind spots, that are outside of our awareness yet cause us to attribute characteristics to particular groups of people (Banaji & Greenwald, 2013).

Such blind spots can get in the way of our ability to authentically engage with others who are different from us, and can contribute to underrepresented groups feeling like they don't belong. They also make it difficult not only to empathize with people who we think are different from ourselves, but hinder our ability to work well with others and to learn and grow from interactions with those around us. For example, perhaps a child who is a newcomer to the United States joins a typical public-school classroom in that country. English may not be their first language, and their English-speaking classmates may at first believe that there is no way for them to become friends or connect with one another. However, we have all probably seen the ways that language differences can break down in the face of social connections like playing a game, such as soccer or basketball together. What once felt like an insurmountable barrier to connection and friendship can be overcome when we find things that we enjoy doing together.

The good news is, once we can identify our blind spots and know how they alter our perceptions, then we can learn to change our behavior and connect with folks from many different backgrounds (Banaji & Greenwald, 2013).

Conversation starter

All human brains make connections. Many times, we make connections to prior learning when we encounter something new. Connecting new information to what we already know is a way that we learn, grow, and remember. This subconscious process is one of our brain's most brilliant capabilities. Unfortunately, it also subconsciously makes negative associations with regard to cultural and social biases that are embedded in our culture. To fight against these implicit biases, we must first recognize and acknowledge them.

Let's Get Started:

Without telling your child the goal of this activity, invite your child to draw with you. Ask your child to help you draw four pictures of a frog. Here are the instructions for the four drawings:

- ❍ Draw a frog from the perspective of a fly.
- ❍ Draw a frog from the perspective of a fish.
- ❍ Draw a frog from the perspective of a 7-year-old child.
- ❍ Draw a frog from the perspective of a biology student.

Lay out all four drawings side by side. Lead your child in a conversation about how each picture of a frog looks completely different based on whose perspective was taken.

Taking it to the next level!

Based on the age, maturity, and experience of your child, choose one or more of the following activities to continue thinking about implicit bias.

Unconscious bias is difficult to comprehend for many children because of its abstract nature. The following activities will help create an initial framework in which children can begin to understand biases we might have without even knowing it.

1. Use the Harvard Implicit Bias website and their testing options. For a middle schooler, the initial card sorting activity on the site is a clear introduction to our inability to sort quickly when the sorting does not fit the categories that seem most obvious to us.

2. The second activity is designed to alert a child to the protagonists in their favorite books.

    a. Brainstorm the titles of the most popular fiction books for your child's class or grade.

    b. After brainstorming, help your child list the protagonist for each book beside the title. Discuss how many protagonists are white and how many are non-white. If the list seems inequitable, create a plan to develop a broader list of young adult fiction in which the protagonist is a person of color or person from another underrepresented group.

3. Read Aesop's fable of the tortoise and the hare. Guide your child in a discussion about what assumptions the hare made about the tortoise. How did those assumptions affect how the hare viewed the tortoise? What choices did the hare make based on those assumptions? Connect these assumptions to assumptions made in society about various groups of people (people in wheelchairs, people who are very short, people who haven't attended college, etc.).

References

Applebaum, B. (2019). Remediating campus climate: Implicit bias training is not enough. *Studies in Philosophy and Education, 38,* 129-141. https://doi.org/10.1007/s!!217-018-9644-1.

Banaji, M. R., & Greenwald, A. G. (2013). Blindspot : hidden biases of good people. Delacorte Press.

Bias and Worldview

Question: How can we help children and adolescents identify bias in media?

Overview: In this content, we will think about how parents can help children consider how various viewpoints shape the messages that are conveyed in the media. They will learn how to spot bias in the media they consume. The Extension activity will introduce children to the concept of worldview and why it is important to consider when consuming media.

What does the research tell us about bias?

All of us have a distinctive worldview that colors the way we see and thus interpret the world around us. A worldview is simply the lens through which we view the world, the assumptions that we make about truth, value, and humanity. As we discussed in looking at implicit bias, biases can influence the way that we see the world and both understand and interact with those around us. That's important to keep in mind as we explore the concept of both our own worldview and those of the makers of the media that we consume.

The people who develop media and marketing campaigns have their own worldviews. Their perspective will influence the programs and products that they develop. On top of that, these campaigns are promoting consumption. The point behind them is to sell something, so of course they will work to make consumers feel that they need it, whether it is a beauty product or the latest electronic gadget.

Whenever an author of a book, television show, advertisement or movie creates a piece of media, they are sharing their own worldview whether blatantly or subtly. For example, in some television shows, one sees a consistent dichotomy of a smart, sassy girl compared to a goofy, bumbling boy or a wise cracking, funny wife who has to put up with her dim-witted husband. In other movies or television shows, successful men may be presented as emotionally distant and cold or high-status women may be depicted as hard to get along with and demanding. These themes are conspicuous enough to be picked up on by the tweens and teens who consume this media. If children are consistently consuming media that perpetuates a specific worldview about where an individual's value lies or what kinds of interests or traits one is expected to have based on gender, race or some other point of identity, then they will begin to be impacted by that worldview. This is important because the worldview shapes a student's understanding of who they are and what makes them valuable.

When children begin to understand that each piece of media or marketing that they consume has been crafted to promote a particular perspective, they can learn to identify that perspective and ask themselves how they feel about it. Do they agree or disagree with the worldview presented?

Recognizing that worldview exists, identifying the worldview or bias of the source of the message, and comparing that worldview to one's own all lead to the development of critical media literacy skills that allow the child to become an active, critical consumer.

Conversation starter

It's easy to forget that our own perspective creates a worldview that becomes the lens through which we view the world. The colloquial term for this is "perspectacle." This word combines "perspective" with "spectacles," imagining that we put on our "glasses"—the lens through which we view the world around us. Our own biases shape that view further. Our culture often discusses worldview and bias as a negative, but when we are willing to acknowledge that each person has a worldview colored with various biases, then those words are normalized and neutralized. Recognizing our own worldview(s) and biases allows us to be more self-aware and to empathize with others.

Let's get started!

- ❍ Select ahead of time video clips that demonstrate bias. Two suggestions are "Don Cherry—on women at hockey games" on YouTube and "FOX news host attacks Muslim scholar who wrote about Jesus (Reza Aslan)." The first one is about sports and the second one is about religions. If unable to locate these exact clips, find a suitable substitute to demonstrate bias in reporting.
- ❍ To begin this time with your child, ask them to define bias. Check to see what their understanding is of this term as you enter this conversation.
- ❍ After showing them the video clips, ask your child what bias they might have noticed.
- ❍ Now you and your child will choose a couple of current events you are interested in and/or know about to some extent. Once you have chosen your current events, talk about the various "sides" of these events and how these "sides" might create a biased reporting of the story. Example: the NBA finals as reported by one team's public affairs representative, or by a local news source for the other team.

- As noted in the "Conversation starter," the idea of bias often is perceived negatively. To push back on that notion, ask your child the following questions: Is bias always negative? Why is it important to recognize bias in the media and in ourselves?
- Ask your child to choose the current event they are most interested in. Then work with them to create a story/report from the perspective of a completely unbiased reporter. Example: An unbiased story about current presidential candidates, or about a mainstream band losing one of its members, or about the NBA finals.
- Once this story is completed, interrogate your story with the following questions:
  - Does the story give more than one viewpoint?
  - Is there information that might be left out?
  - Is it free of emotionally charged words/phrases or identifying a group mentality (working class, unwed mothers, teenage drivers, etc)?
  - Did the story avoid extremes (worst/best, highest/lowest)?
- Discuss with your child the challenge of news reporting remaining as bias free as possible.

Take it to the next level!

The concept of worldview is abstract and difficult even for adults, so to ask preteens and young teenagers to consider their own worldview is a tall order. That said, many gifted children have already wrestled with deeper ideas like worldview well before their age peers. This opportunity to take it to the next level is definitely most suited to children who are willing and eager to think deeply about personal matters and will be able to be self-reflective.

A basic definition of worldview is how one looks at the world, how one thinks it operates, why things happen the way they do, and what one's purpose is. Make sure your child understands the concept of worldview. Ask them to write about their own worldview for five minutes. If your child seems stuck by this request, offer the following reminders of elements of worldview:

- What are one's beliefs about God/Higher Power?
- What makes up a family?
- How does a good person act and engage with the world?
- What makes a good community (city, civic organization, country, etc.)?

The goal of this five minutes is to keep writing. Tell the child that formatting, spelling, punctuation do not matter. Ask them not to edit themselves, but rather to write what comes to their mind like journaling. This generative writing may feel quite private to them. You could assure them that you will not read what they wrote, and they will only share it with you if they choose.

After they have completed writing for five minutes, reflect on the following questions. Both you and your child should respond!

- What media do you consume regularly that affirms your worldview?
- What media do you consume that represents a different worldview?
- Does the worldview that media portrays matter? Why or why not?
- Do the digital media messages you create (social media, videos, etc) reflect your worldview? Should they?

References

Renee R. Hobbs, Digital and Media Literacy: Connecting Culture and Classroom (Thousand Oaks, CA: Corwin Press, 2011).

Stereotypes and Halo Effect

Question: How can we teach children to recognize stereotyping in the media?

Overview: In this section we will look at how parents can help children understand stereotypes presented in the media and how those influence a child's understanding of expectations based on standards in their own culture. We will also consider gender stereotypes prevalent in advertising and marketing. The activities will give children practice in identifying stereotypes and halo effects. Stereotypes tend to be fixed and often oversimplified image or idea about a particular type of person or thing while halo effect is more specifically how one's positive impression on a person, group, product, brand, etc. positively influences one's opinions or feelings in another area. We'll take it to the next level by looking with children at advertising messages about gender.

What does the research tell us about stereotyping and halo effects?

Media messages affect a child's understanding of themselves and their place in the world. They shape and define an adolescent's idea of acceptable appearance and behavior. To figure out where he or she falls on the continuum of acceptability, the child will compare her or himself to social models that are presented as ideal. The mass media in general has been identified as a particularly potent purveyor of ideal behavior and appearance (Bell & Dittmar, 2011), and adolescents are particularly vulnerable to using celebrities and media depictions as social models (Groesz, Levine & Murnen, 2002). One need look no further than children sporting the jersey of their favorite sports celebrity and aspiring to be just like them when they grow up.

As you think about your child and their engagement with media, it's important to know that people who identify more strongly with media characters and celebrities and who have already developed concerns about their own appearance are more likely to be impacted negatively by stereotyped media images (Bell & Dittmar, 2011; Want, 2009).

What is the halo effect?

The halo effect is a cognitive bias where the perception of one trait, or characteristic of a person or object, is influenced by information about another, often irrelevant trait (Forgas & Laham, 2009). For example, I may meet a tall man and think he is good at basketball. In this case, the man's tallness is leading me to assume that he is a good basketball player, even though I have no information about how or if he plays sports. An early adolescent may see popular characters on their favorite shows or social media wearing certain clothing or engaging in risky behaviors and assume that to be popular they must follow suit.

As children grow, they begin to understand stereotypes in a more complex way and may be able to be more aware of halo effects. For example, both halo effects and stereotypes are often linked to gender. By the time they are about seven, children expand their ideas of gender to include personality traits and academic achievement as well as physical characteristics. We know that adults tend to describe more desirable traits such as leadership skills, ambition, self-confidence, and independence as masculine and less desirable traits, such as being emotional, needing approval, getting feelings hurt easily, and passivity as feminine traits (Powlishta, 2000). Children have been shown to think about such traits as linked to gender as well.

In early elementary school, children even begin to think about certain academic subjects as masculine or feminine. For example, language and performing arts tend to be more strongly associated with females while mathematics and sciences are more strongly associated with males. Interestingly, stereotypes also impact the way that children rate their own abilities in an area. For example, a girl with high math ability is more likely to rate her abilities lower than a boy with the same math ability would (Bhanat & Jovanovic, 2005).

Do advertisements promote stereotypes?

Television commercials for children overwhelmingly present gender stereotypes. For example, in commercials we'll see pastel colors, cooperation, and indoor play associated primarily with girls and competition and outdoor play associated with boys (Kahlenberg & Hein, 2010). Johnson and Young (2002) examined the themes of gendered voice and words present in children's television commercials. In looking at these, they saw clear gender patterns in the types of verbs that were used in commercials featuring the different genders. Action, competition, and destruction words, such as break, flip, hit, smash, transform and construct, were used most often in advertisements that featured boys and boy-targeted products. Verbs that focused on limited activity, feelings, and nurturing, such as look, see, wait, cuddle, and caring, were used most often in advertisements that featured girls and girl-targeted products.

Another pattern that was found involved the use of verbs of agency or control. These words were found more often in boy-oriented advertisements than girl-oriented advertisements, with a ratio of more than 4:1. This study also examined the ways that boys and girls spoke in advertisements aimed at children. In advertisements that were targeting both girls and boys, boys spoke more, and girls often spoke only in response to the actions or statements of boys. When we consider the use of the word "power" and related words, 21% of boy-oriented advertisements used the words "power" or "powerful," but in all of the girl-oriented advertisements, there was only one incident of the word "power" being used, and it was in the context of identifying the maker of a Barbie car (Power Wheels) (Johnson & Young, 2002). The authors conclude, "Toy makers and their advertisers either make no effort to associate or may consciously avoid associating girl-toys with power or their potential to transfer power to their users" (Johnson & Young, 2002). Even in educational software, you see over and over that boys are represented as aggressive, active, and competitive while girls are dependent and passive (Sheldon, 2004). When children repeatedly see these gender stereotypes, they begin to believe them.

Conversation starter

Stereotypes are all around us. They can be tricky because many stereotypes are based in a small sliver of truth which causes us to buy into them so easily. For example, in the NBA, there are men who are often much taller than the average man, so, as noted previously, when a child immediately thinks a very tall man is a basketball player, that thought is based on information that is not inaccurate. The difference is that not **all** very tall men play basketball, of course! Helping children process stereotypes and how they can be harmful is a positive step in becoming a savvier media consumer.

Let's get started!

- ❍ Over the course of several days or weeks, make a practice of pointing out characters in books, TV shows, movies, and online content who have extreme physical characteristics. Note those who are extremely beautiful, unattractive, severe, overweight, etc.
- ❍ As you casually note the characters' physical traits, wonder aloud with your child what that person's character might be.
- ❍ If your child is willing, ask them what made them assign certain character traits to the various individuals in the book or media you are considering.
- ❍ Discuss halo effect and why it is detrimental and sets many people up for immediate failure and others up for success with no basis in reality.
- ❍ Think with your child how halo effect and stereotyping are alike and different.
- ❍ Ask them if they have ever been stereotyped. If so, when was it and how did it feel?
- ❍ Come up with 3-4 questions with your child to stop and ask yourself to avoid falling into the trap of stereotyping.

Take it to the next level!

If you choose to continue the conversation, this section will zoom in and consider specific gender stereotyping. Culture assigns traits to little girls and little boys and your child likely has noticed this. This activity seeks to break down traditional gender stereotypes by pretending to market to a wider audience.

1. Guide a conversation with your child about how products are marketed to boys and girls based on gender stereotypes. Topics for consideration might be books, bedroom decor, toys, and graphic T-shirts.

2. You could explore online shopping sites for evidence of these stereotypes. Look at advertising from various retailers for examples.

3. Make a list of your findings either verbally or on paper.

4. Help your child create an advertisement for a product that opposes cultural gender stereotypes. Encourage them to use words and images.

References

Bell, B., & Dittmar, H. (2011). Does Media Type Matter? The Role of Identification in Adolescent Girls' Media Consumption and the Impact of Different Thin-Ideal Media on Body Image. Sex Roles, 65(7–8), 478–490. https://doi.org/10.1007/s11199-011-9964-x

Bhanot, R. & Jovanovic, J. (2005). "Do Parents' Academic Gender Stereotypes Influence Whether They Intrude on their Children's Homework?" Sex Roles 52, no. 9-10, pp. 597-607.

Forgas, J. P., & Laham, S. (2009). Halo effects. In R. Baumeister, & K. D. Vohs (Eds.), Encyclopedia of social psychology (pp. 499—502). Thousand Oaks : Sage Publications.

Groesz, L.M., Levine, M.P. and Murnen, S.K. (2002). "The Effect of Experimental Presentation of Thin Media Images on Body Satisfaction: A Meta-analytic Review." International Journal Of Eating Disorders 31, 1: 1-16.

Johnson, F.L. & Young, K. (2002). "Gendered Voices in Children's Television Advertising." Critical Studies In Media Communication 19, 4, pp. 461-477.

Kahlenberg, S. & Hein, M. "Progression on Nickelodeon? Gender-Role Stereotypes in Toy Commercials." Sex Roles 62, no. 11/12 (2010): 830-847.

Powlishta, K. K. (2000), "The Effect of Target Age on the Activation of Gender Stereotypes." Sex Roles 42, no. 3/4: 271-282.

Sheldon, J.P. (2004). "Gender Stereotypes in Educational Software for Young Children." Sex Roles 51, no. 7/8, pg. 433-444.

Want, S. C., (2009). "Meta-analytic Moderators of Experimental Exposure to Media Portrayals of Women on Female Appearance Satisfaction: Social Comparisons as Automatic Processes." Body Image 6, no. 4: 257-269.

Permanence of Generating Online Content

Question: How can parents help their children understand the permanence of the things that they post online and make wise decisions about their digital footprint?

Overview: In this section, we'll talk about how to help children think ethically about how they interact with those they know in real life and with online strangers. The activities will help children think about their online reputation and the permanence of content created in online spaces.

What does the research say about our digital footprints?

Today's tween and teenagers have "grown up digital" (Tapscott, 1997), with their communication practices, ethics, and identity shaped by their interactions with and use of digital media (James, 2014; Flores & James, 2012). From their comfort level in using digital media to share information to their knowledge of world events and popular culture, adolescents use digital media in many ways. According to recent research (Rideout & Robb, 2019), the average amount of time that teens spend on social media each day is just over an hour (1 hour 10 minutes). The frequency of use has increased over the past five years, with 63% of teens saying they use social media everyday compared to 45% in 2015. About 41% of teens reported enjoying social media "a lot." It is important for parents to note that the median age that teens reported beginning to use social media is 14. Some children may start using social media much earlier while others may do so a bit later.

If your children aren't already using social media, they likely will begin to do so fairly soon. So, this is a great time to help them begin to think about the concept of digital reputation management, or how to be purposeful in the digital footprint that they leave. We need to give children opportunities to think about how their behavior online might impact others and its long-term impact on their own reputation.

There are both benefits and challenges for tweens and teens navigating social media. They have the opportunity to connect with new people and learn new things, but also the potential to harm others and to be harmed themselves. That harm can come not from an intention to hurt others, but from what James (2014) says is "a failure to consider the potential effects of one's actions on other people, known and unknown" (James, 2014, pg. 3). James (2014) calls these failures blind spots, and this section is designed to help children uncover those blind spots, begin to consider and anticipate the potential effects of their own social media behavior, and come to understand the permanence of digital artifacts and how those may impact themselves or others long term. James recommends that we focus on helping children develop ethical "ways of thinking" that consider the good of three groups: self, known others and others in a larger community.

In working with children to develop ethical thinking with these three groups in mind, James (2014) suggests three forms of thinking. These are:

1. Thinking about roles and responsibilities, with a focus on developing awareness of the commitments that the student has in existing relationships (e.g., family, clubs, friendships).

2. Complex perspective taking, or learning to think about how one's own online behaviors might affect multiple different people, for example, family members, friends or teachers.

3. Community thinking, considering the potential harms and benefits to larger groups, such as school, city, or other groups.

As children begin to develop these ways of thinking, they will become more effective digital citizens who are able to consider the effects of their use of digital media and develop an understanding of how to best manage their own online reputation.

Conversation starter

All of us have said something that we immediately regret and wish we could take back. Once we say something out loud, we certainly can apologize or seek to make things right if needed, but what's been said is still said! The same is true of online content, but often we don't think of it in the same way. We are so accustomed to scrolling on by that we forget any comment, post, or other online content is staying right where we typed it.

Let's get started!

- ❍ Purchase an inexpensive tube of toothpaste and have paper towels on hand.
- ❍ Encourage your child to squeeze out ALL of the toothpaste onto a paper towel.
- ❍ Join them in trying to get ALL the toothpaste back into the tube. You will quickly realize it's impossible!
- ❍ Without further discussing the toothpaste activity, brainstorm together some funny and cryptic online names someone could have. For example: jwsmithboy, balletbeauty12, junkfoodmillionaire, etc.
- ❍ Ask your child if they've ever seen someone post on a social media platform and receive hateful or mean comments. Discuss why this might happen.
- ❍ Show your child the pretend post and photo The post is a picture of a teenager who has colored her hair green with the following text: "omg. I did it! I h8 u @baseballkiller! U said green would luk bad but ha! I luk awesome!"

- Using the pretend online names, make up comments that this individual might make in response to the green hair girl's post. If your child tries to stay polite, throw in some uncomfortable or mean comments to make the activity most effective.
- Choose one of the harshest comments as an example. Wonder aloud who might see that response…someone looking to hire the commenter for a job? A potential romantic partner? A potential university they hope to attend? The toothpaste is out of the tube, and it cannot be put back in! Online content is a permanent fixture even if a person goes back to delete comments because the comments could have already been saved through a screenshot.
- Show the video or written story (https://www.nytimes.com/2015/02/15/magazine/how-one-stupid-tweet-ruined-justine-saccos-life.html) about a woman (Justine Sacco) traveling to Africa having tweeted about AIDS and by the time she arrives in Africa, her twitter account has exploded, and she has lost her job.
- Spur further discussion on how being anonymous sometimes gives us false security to say things we might not say in person or with our name attached.

Take it to the next level!

Chat with your child about their future goals for college and their professional life. Many children at this age will only have a vague notion of what they might want to do for college or for a profession, but most gifted children often know they want to go to a certain type of college and have dreams of a career even if their plans are not fully formed. Share with your child that in many college applications and applications for internships, letters of recommendation are needed. Ask them to think of an adult they trust who could write a letter of recommendation for them in the future. They will then pretend to write the letter they hope that adult might write on their behalf. In other words, they will write a letter that reflects how they hope a trusted adult will view them someday. After the letter is completed, talk more about how social media content might affect someone's ability to recommend a student for college, an internship, or a job. What kind of social media content might reflect poorly on someone's character? What types of social media content might show a person's positive traits? Discuss some personal guidelines for posting on social media based on how they hope others will view them.

References

James, C. (2014). Disconnected : Youth, New Media, and the Ethics Gap. The MIT Press.

Rideout, V., and Robb, M. B. (2019). The Common Sense census: Media use by tweens and teens, 2019. San Francisco, CA: Common Sense Media.

Tapscott, D. (1997). Growing up Digital. Informationweek, 655, 64.

Being an Active Consumer

Question: How can parents help their children learn to judge the purpose, intent, audience, and values of various media messages?

Overview: In this section, children will consider the importance of being an active consumer of media rather than passively letting media come to them. We'll also give you the chance to take a deep look at the complicated topic of fake news and other misleading types of media.

What does the research tell us about the importance of being an active consumer?

Throughout this book, we have used the bioecological model as a lens to understand child development. We've focused on the interactions between the child as an active learner within their environment. The important thing to remember about this perspective is that rather than being a passive consumer of media, the child is powerful and active. The approach of teaching children to become critical consumers of media is vital. In this section, we will share strategies to engage youth in actively examining media in a way that allows them to enjoy and learn from it. And we'll share examples of both positive portrayals and ones that may be perceived as more negative to give children a chance to consider both.

Bronfenbrenner viewed the process of development as one in which the child can learn to fit into the existing environment and those expectations, but can also change their environment through their own actions (Bronfenbrenner, 1979, 1992, 2005, Bronfenbrenner

& Morris, 1998; 2006). When we give children the tools to critique and challenge messages from media and marketing, they can become change makers. They learn that their actions can lead to change in their environment.

Whenever an author of a book, television show, or movie creates a piece for media, they are sharing their own worldview and values. We've already talked about the fact that if children are consistently consuming media that perpetuates a specific worldview or value, then they will likely begin to be impacted by that worldview. In this section of the book, we want to learn how to support our children in learning how to develop their own worldview based on their individual and community beliefs and values and how to compare the worldviews presented through popular media to their own.

The way that children learn to engage with, interpret, and respond to media messages is mediated by different variables within their lives. The bioecological systems within a child's life, including their own unique characteristics as well as the microsystems of family, school, and community and the macrosystem of larger culture provide a child with assets or challenges to effectively respond to media. With the help of caring adults, children can learn how to process and evaluate media messages on their own terms.

When adolescents begin to understand that each media message or marketing that they consume has been crafted to promote a particular perspective, they can learn to identify that perspective and ask themselves how they feel about it. Do they agree or disagree with the worldview presented? When we see our children as empowered consumers and creators, we give them the chance to identify their own power in making informed choices.

Adolescents themselves are great advocates for their perspective because they are at a particular stage of development when their power to resist peer pressure is growing (Pfeifer, Masten, Moore, Oswald, Mazziotta, Iacoboni & Dapretto, 2011). Many adolescents are hungry to make a difference in the world, to be world changers. By harnessing that energy and giving them tools to become critical media consumers, caregivers can lend them a hand in learning to critically evaluate media and marketing campaigns. Using social media and word of mouth, adolescents and caring adults can work together to advocate for healthy behaviors and worldviews.

Conversation starter

Over the course of a week or two, take a picture of your family members watching TV or spending time online (phone, computer, iPad, etc.). Consuming online or television content quickly becomes a fully passive activity where the consumer is just taking in the content without thinking about it much at all. These kinds of photos always reveal the level of blank consumption happening when consuming media! This activity is designed to challenge this!

Let's get started!

- ❍ Choose a show with your child that you both would enjoy.
- ❍ Watch a couple episodes free of conversation.
- ❍ After a few episodes, ask them what questions they ask of themselves as they are watching. Chances are you will receive a blank look!
- ❍ Introduce the five questions by Renee Hobbs that can be asked to be a more active than passive media consumer.
    - Who is the creator of the piece and what is its purpose?
    - How does the creator of the piece attract and hold your attention?
    - What lifestyles, values, and worldviews are represented?
    - How might different people interpret this message?
    - What is left out?
- ❍ At a later time (not associated with that particular show), remind them of the effects of media consumption:
    - Can be addictive
    - Makes us compare our lives with others
    - Makes us restless
    - Gives rise to cyberbullying
    - Glamorizes risky behavior
    - Can make us dissatisfied
    - Can make us feel left out

- If you and/or your child watch a variety of shows on TV or online, make a list of the shows you enjoy watching separately or together.
- Make a list of products your child really likes.
- Create a list of short videos of advertisements of their favorite products and clips from their favorite shows.
- Watch the short video clips using Hobbs' questions above to interrogate the content.
- Asking these questions makes us active consumers of media, not passive consumers. Discuss with them what happens when we passively consume media. We often see something that is NOT there or don't see something clearly. As an example, show the Dove commercial from YouTube titled "Dove Evolution" in which a one-minute video shows how a regular woman is altered using make-up, hair changes, and then digital enhancements. After seeing this video, my (Amy) own son noted that the woman on the billboard "doesn't even exist." In other words, sometimes what we see is far from reality and passive media consumption allows us to not even consider this possibility.
- Discuss with your child how you view media messages differently when you are an active consumer rather than a passive one. Explore why actively consuming is healthier. In this conversation, you could include the way we view ourselves, products we buy, stereotypes we accept, etc. What changes would be needed in your media consumption habits to become a more active consumer rather than passively allowing media messages to soak into your mind?

Take it to the next level!

An increasingly important part of being an active consumer of media is recognizing fake news. A child's view of the concept of fake news will vary depending on their parents/caregivers' perspective on news sources, bias, politics, and level of trust of media in general. The following activities provide ways to spot fake news.

Many children might believe that fake news is any news that paints a public figure or public situation they like in a poor light. Fake news, by definition, is false/untrue, junk news, pseudo-news, hoax news, alternative facts, misleading content, or deliberate misinformation.

Begin by asking your child if they believe they can spot fake news or fake information online easily. Show them the following websites and have a discussion about which of these might be real and which might be fake.

- Website about best hunting dogs by the American Kennel Club
- http://www.dhmo.org/: This website is a fake site created to show children how easy it is to look "real" and be fake.
- The US Government site about how Senators are elected: https://www.senate.gov/artandhistory/history/common/briefing/Direct_Election_Senators.htm

Once your child sees that it is easy to be fooled by online content, explore some of the terms often used in the conversation about fake news. Look up each of the following terms to define and provide an example: clickbait, propaganda, satire/parody, misleading headlines, biased/slanted news, editorial/opinion pieces. An extra topic would be sloppy journalism, but it is harder to define quickly and more challenging to find quick examples. By the end of this exercise, they will be knowledgeable about all the terms.

After they have a better understanding of the relevant terms/topics, introduce them to the simple acronym for checking to see if a source is worth considering. The acronym is CRAAP.

- Currency: is the information current
- Relevancy: is the information relevant for your particular reason for searching
- Authority: does the author of the information have the authority or expertise to write competently on the topic

- Accuracy: is the information reliable, truthful, or correct based on evidence or peer review and is the information free from technical errors like spelling, grammar, punctuation
- Purpose: what is the reason this information exists in this location

There are multiple checklists online that children can use to move through the CRAAP Test if this is helpful. Knowing how to do this will benefit them throughout their school career as they conduct research, too.

Introduce children to fact-checking websites. There are several to choose from. At the writing of this book, some of the options are politifact.com, factcheck.org, and snopes.com.

Using what they've now learned, revisit the three websites above and think about how they would now see them with their new ability to evaluate online content.

References

Bronfenbrenner, U. (1979). The Ecology of Human Development (Cambridge, MA: Harvard University Press, 1979)

Bronfenbrenner, U. (1992). Six Theories of Child Development: Revised Formulations and Current Issues, ed. Ross Vasta (London: Jessica Kingsley) 187-249.

Bronfenbrenner, U. (2005). Making Human Beings Human (Thousand Oaks, CA: Sage).

Bronfenbrenner, U. & Morris, P. A. (1998). "The Ecology of Developmental Processes," in Theoretical Models of Human Development, ed. Richard M. Lerner, vol. 1 of Handbook of Child Psychology, 5th ed., ed. William Damon (New York: Wiley, 1998), 993-1028;

Bronfenbrenner, U. & Morris, P. A. (2006). "The Bioecological Model of Human Development," in Theoretical Models of Human Development, ed. Richard M. Lerner, vol. 1 of Handbook of Child Psychology, 5th ed., ed. William Damon (New York: Wiley).

Jennifer H. Pfeifer, Carrie L. Masten, III, William E. Moore, Tasha M. Oswald, John C. Mazziotta, Marco Iacoboni, and Mirella Dapretto. "Entering Adolescence: Resistance to Peer Influence, Risky Behavior, and Neural Changes in Emotion Reactivity." Neuron 69 (2011): 1029-1036.

Celebrity Culture

Objective: In their study of celebrity culture, children will analyze the lives of celebrities and judge why their lives create meaning/value for culture.

Question: How can caregivers help children analyze celebrity culture and come to understand the value that different people bring to society, individually and as a whole?

Overview: This section will focus on how celebrities in the media influence our values and personal lifestyle beliefs. Celebrities often hold great influence and power over those who follow them closely. Their words and actions are often magnified and elevated as having greater importance than someone who is not famous or well-known. The activities in this section will guide children to remember that celebrity is often fleeting and is not the most stable footing on which to place one's values. The activities guide children to consider why a particular person is famous. They also help children evaluate whether the values they hold personally align with the values presented by the celebrity.

What does the research say about celebrity culture?

In this session we will explore the different ways that celebrities influence children and adolescents through various media. Children and adolescents are in the process of constructing their identity, and media is one of the forces they use to help them figure out who they are, who they want to be, and who they think they should be.

Adolescents are active media users. They do not simply soak up media content, but instead make sense of it from their own individual perspective and experience. For many adolescents, celebrities serve as social role models. This idea is linked with social comparison theory, which says that people compare themselves to others and strive to get social rewards, like attention and popularity, by copying those who have achieved higher social status.

Adolescents use celebrities as social models to which they compare themselves. In fact, Giles (2004) claims that one of the most important psychological influences of media for adolescents is the forming of what he calls "parasocial" relationships with celebrities.

As adolescents are forming their own identity, their use of celebrities as comparison figures leads them to look to the celebrity for guidance on values, attitudes, and behaviors, including negative behaviors (Giles & Maltby, 2004; North, Sheridan, Maltby, & Gillett, 2007). Involvement with celebrities in general has been shown to influence adolescents in their purchasing behavior, attitudes, and behavioral choices (Chia & Poo, 2009). As we help our children consider celebrity culture, we will give them the opportunity to think about the concept of fame and celebrity itself as well as their own response to it.

Conversation starter

More than ever, tweens and teens look to online personalities as role models. In this specific moment in time, those in the media to whom others look are even called "influencers!" Ask your child what makes someone an influencer. Ask them how they would define celebrity. What does a person have to do to be considered a celebrity? The answers to these questions have certainly evolved!

Let's get started!

- ❍ Begin by thinking back about yourself when you were your child's age. Who were the people you looked to as celebrities? Who were the famous singers? Actors? Bands?
- ❍ Look up 4-6 of these former celebrities and screenshot each on your phone.
- ❍ Invite your child into a conversation and tell them you have some photos of people you'd like to share with them.
- ❍ Show them each former celebrity picture and ask if they know who that person is.
- ❍ Most likely, most will be unfamiliar or unknown to your child.
- ❍ Ask them which celebrities they follow the most closely and why. Wonder aloud what these celebrities might be doing in 10, 20, 30 years.
- ❍ Continue the conversation that may naturally unfold that celebrity is often fleeting even though in the moment a celebrity seems so important.
- ❍ Discuss fame. What is it? Is fame something to strive for? What values and lifestyles do they represent? Are these lifestyles and values reflected in your own goals and values?

Take it to the next level!

Your child has now considered celebrity culture and their own values and lifestyle goals. You and your child will now keep a journal of media interaction as self-reflection to check if your stated values and lifestyle goals align with your media interaction.

Before beginning the journaling exercise, help your child to identify their own personal values and lifestyle goals including, but not limited to: fairness, justice, religious beliefs, inclusiveness, being a good friend, following rules, being a good student, and how they spend their time. Consider your own personal values, too.

For one week (or longer if necessary or desired), each of you will answer the following items in a journal at the end of each day:

- ❍ How many minutes did I engage with media of any kind today?
- ❍ List 1-3 things you saw or heard today in any of the media you engaged that affirmed your personal values or lifestyle goals.
- ❍ List 1-3 things you saw or heard today in any of the media you engaged that opposed your personal values or lifestyle goals.

At the end of the week (or more), reflect together on how your media choices align with your personal values or beliefs. If your media choices do not reflect your values, brainstorm goals that would adjust your media interaction to better align with your values.

References

Giles, D. C., & Maltby, J. j. (2004). The role of media figures in adolescent development: Relations between autonomy, attachment, and interest in celebrities. Personality & Individual Differences, 36(4), 813. doi:10.1016/S0191-8869(03)00154-5

North, A. C., Sheridan, L., Maltby, J., & Gillett, R. (2007). Attributional style, self-esteem, and celebrity worship. Media Psychology, 9(2), 291-308. doi:10.1080/15213260701285975

Chia, S. C., & Yip Ling, P. (2009). Media, celebrities, and fans: An examination of adolescents' media usage and involvement with entertainment celebrities. Journalism & Mass Communication Quarterly, 86(1), 23-44.

Data Literacy

Question: What is Big Data and why is it important for us to understand?

Overview: This section will introduce children to the abstract concept that their internet searches are providing personal data for various companies and groups.

What does the research say about big data?

Every time we get online, we are generating data that can and is used to understand us and our behaviors. Whether it's what we buy or search for online, or whose images and posts we like on social media, data is being collected and organized. Every time we sign up to receive discounts or information, we're sharing our own data with companies that are putting it together to keep track of who we are in terms of age, gender, and geographical location, and what we are interested in purchasing or learning about. This information is called Big Data. As Grassegger and Krogerus (2017) explain, Big Data means that everything we do on and offline creates digital traces. All that information is stored and can be used by those who want to sell us something and those who want to manipulate our behavior.

As we share our phone numbers, email addresses and names, third party data brokers are working across platforms to connect the dots between all of our different online activities and both our online and offline interests (Fontichiaro, 2019). Many people, both children and adults, don't understand that their online activity is being monitored and collected as data in order to develop a full digital picture of them as an individual.

Children may think it's no big deal if their data is gathered for advertisements. After all, maybe it's a good thing for companies to know what they're looking to buy. Maybe that information leads them to bigger discounts. But it's important for all of us to understand that data isn't just gathered to sell us things, but to manage and manipulate our behavior in both big and small ways. For example, in 2016 a total of 87 million Facebook users, most of them in the United States, completed a quiz called "thisisyourdigitallife" that allowed Cambridge Analytica to gather information about them (Confessore, 2018). Cambridge Analytica then used this information to identify gullible voters in both the United States and the United Kingdom and created targeted misleading political advertisements to those voters in order to manipulate them to vote for the candidates who had hired them (Confessore, 2018; Grasseger & Krogerus, 2017). Many believe that both the 2016 U.S. election and the Brexit referendum in the United Kingdom were heavily influenced by the use of Big Data to target voters.

According to recent research, the analytics techniques used for big data are now commonly put to work through Social Network Analysis (SNA) to identify patterns of communication among users. This digital data collected via social media can be used to monitor group and individual behavior, and that may have big repercussions in our lives (Bazzaz Abkenar et al., 2021). For example, in August 2019, 17-year-old Ismail B. Ajjawi was all set to begin his first year at Harvard. However, when he landed in Boston, Custom and Border Protection agents searched his computer and smartphone and found what they deemed anti-American social media posts from connections of his. Ismail's visa was then canceled, and he was denied entry into the United States (Zraick & Zaveri, 2019).

People also have gotten fired from their jobs for offensive posts on social media. A 2015 *Rolling Stone* magazine article shared 17 stories of people who had lost their jobs over social media posts, with posts ranging from British bankers recreating an ISIS beheading to a hospital employee who advocated the indiscriminate shooting of crowds of protestors calling for racial equality (Halper, 2015). College students have had their offers of admissions rescinded from both private and public colleges and universities due to racist posts on social media. Some of these students were penalized for posts that had been created a year or two before their admissions into the institution (Levin, 2020).

All of these incidents make it clear why it is so important for children to build data literacy in order to understand how their online activity generates Big Data and how that data can be used.

Conversation starter

Most tweens and teens have had the experience of searching for a topic online and then immediately seeing advertisements and articles about that topic. It can feel so jarring! However, do they understand what is really going on? This section seeks to peek behind the curtain of big data and how a person's online habits affect what they are shown.

Let's get started!

- ❍ Choose one of the profiles provided in this section.
- ❍ Ask your child to pretend that they're trying to market to the individual described in their profile. They will brainstorm some ideas of companies who might advertise to this person, groups for which that person might be interested, and other organizations of interest.
- ❍ Consider how various companies, organizations, or groups might market to the person described in the profile. Use the following questions for conversation:
  - Is this practice negative? Positive? Both? How?
  - Why is it important to understand how people are targeted through one's online footprint?
  - If a platform or online tool is free to use, how are they making money? How is advertising used? Is it overt on the platform? Or is your collected data sold to advertisers?
  - Could stored personal data be used for nefarious purposes? Could someone pretend to be you to make a purchase or gain access to a school/activity? Could personal information fall into the hands of a predator?
  - How can a person's awareness of a digital footprint help make one more intentional about their own media production and consumption?

Take it to the next level!

Now that your child has considered the mostly-hidden concept of stored personal data and how it is used, they will have the opportunity to think like a company or group wanting to target an individual based on that individual's likes and preferences.

Help your child find a friend (peer or adult) who would be willing to participate in this activity. Ask this person to fill out the information form (included in this section). Go over the person's answers with your child once it is returned to you.

Based on the answers on the information form, your child will create a plan to market and attract the attention of the person who filled out the form. Encourage your child to think broadly and creatively. They can write a narrative. They can include drawings or images that might be used to market to this person. The following questions might be helpful:

- What companies would this person purchase from?
- What businesses could easily overly advertise to this person?
- What groups or organizations would capture this person's attention?
- How could someone market to this person in subtle ways that they might not notice?
- Are there any groups that might seek to do harm that could capture this person's attention?

After your child has completed this activity, invite them to share with the individual who filled out the form.

Profile 1

Mikayla is a 6th grader. She loves sketching, reading fiction books about pioneer days, and playing the piano. She has three sisters. Her family lives in a very small, rural town. She has a dog and a cat. She goes to a small public school with about 40 children in her class. Mikayla has not traveled outside of her city except to visit her grandparents who live an hour away. Her parents are protective of what she watches, so she is only allowed to watch TV shows with her parents. Her time spent online is looking up drawing videos, music videos, and looking for new books to read. She shops at Walmart for clothes and goods. Her parents don't like to support big tech companies like Amazon. Mikayla browses Amazon to read book reviews. Mikayla's parents are fearful of their daughter being exposed to things online that could be dangerous, so they talk frequently about the harmful content that can be on the internet. Mikayla has never experienced anything scary online, so sometimes she secretly searches for some of the topics her parents warn her about to see if they are true. Mikayla isn't allowed to have any social media yet.

Profile 2

James is in 8th grade. James spends hours a day playing online games. Many of the online games involve playing against other people whom he doesn't know in real life. James has had a couple of these people message him privately with concerning questions, but he ignores them. James searches the internet for tips on how to play the online games better. He follows several gamers on YouTube. James lives in a medium-sized city and goes to a private school with little diversity. James' parents are both busy professionals, so they do not monitor his online time closely. He loves shoes and frequently searches online for the newest and best shoes. He aspires to learn how to play the drums so he can be in a band. He follows several drummers online. James loves his hometown's professional hockey team and follows their online presence closely. He also follows the sports teams for the college in his city. James is active on Twitter.

Profile 3

Sierra is about to start high school. She lives in a huge, metropolitan area and her new high school has several thousand children. Sierra has a little brother, and they live with their mom. Sierra's mom works the night shift at a hospital, so Sierra and her brother are often home in the evenings alone. They watch TV together and spend time online scrolling through social media and the internet. Sierra loves to follow Instagram influencers and celebrities. She is interested in lots of actresses and singers. She learns about different fashion designers from the celebrities she follows. She looks up make-up products she learns about. She enjoys watching make-up tutorials on YouTube. Sierra is active on Instagram, Twitter, and Facebook.

Personal Information Form

Name:

Age:

Favorite restaurants:

Favorite places to shop:

2-3 hobbies:

Favorite music:

Favorite brands (clothing, shoes, gadgets, etc.):

Are you a gamer? What games do you play?

What social media platforms do you use?

What are 3 things you browse on YouTube?

What are three things you browse on the internet in general?

What online shopping sites have you bought from?

What kinds of things have you signed up for online recently?

Mailing lists? Business sites? Clubs? Any other places where you have entered personal information like name, address, city, phone number, birthday, age, gender, etc.?

References

Bazzaz Abkenar, S., Haghi Kashani, M., Mahdipour, E., & Jameii, S. M. (2021). Big data analytics meets social media: A systematic review of techniques, open issues, and future directions. Telematics and informatics, 57, 101517. https://doi.org/10.1016/j.tele.2020.101517

Confessore, N. (2018, April 4). Cambridge Analytica and Facebook: The scandal and the fallout so far. Retrieved August 3, 2020 from https://www.nytimes.com/2018/04/04/us/politics/cambridge-analytica-scandal-fallout.html.

Fontichiaro, K. (2019). Data Literacy: Negotiating Convenience and Data Privacy. Teacher Librarian, 47(1), 51–54.

Grassegger, H. & Krogerus, M. (2017, January 28). The data that turned the world upside down. *Vice.* Retrieved August 4, 2020 from https://www.vice.com/en_us/article/mg9vvn/how-our-likes-helped-trump-win.

Halper, K. (2015, July 13). A brief history of people getting fired for social media stupidity. Retrieved August 4, 2020 from https://www.rollingstone.com/culture/culture-lists/a-brief-history-of-people-getting-fired-for-social-media-stupidity-73456/the-bankers-who-think-isis-killings-are-a-hoot-153345.

Levin, D. (2020, July 2). Colleges Rescinding Admissions Offers as Racist Social Media Posts Emerge. Retrieved August 2, 2020 from https://www.nytimes.com/2020/07/02/us/racism-social-media-college-admissions.html.

Zraick, K. & Zaveri, M. (2019, August 27). Harvard children says he was barred from U.S. over his friends' social media posts. *New York Times.* Retrieved August 3, 2020 from https://www.nytimes.com/2019/08/27/us/harvard-student-ismail-ajjawi.html.

Social Media

Question: How can caregivers help children learn to use social media thoughtfully?

Overview: This section will consider the ways that we use social media and how it affects us. We'll also explore the most effective ways to use social media.

What does the research say about social media?

How many of you have social media accounts? Do you tend to check and share from your social media accounts regularly? If so, for you does that mean every day or more than once a day? Recent research has shown that in 2021, 79% of Americans had a social media profile of some kind. That is an increase from the 10% who did so in 2008 and 50% in 2011 (Broadband Search, 2021). This same study noted that the highest percentage of people tend to be using Facebook, then YouTube, followed by Instagram, Twitter, TikTok, and Snapchat (Broadband Search, 2021). A 2019 study showed an increase in teens reporting that they use social media every day, jumping from 45% in 2015 to 63% in 2019 (Rideout & Robb, 2019). A national survey conducted in 2018 noted that 81% of teenagers reported that they used social media, with 70% of those reporting that they use it more than once a day, 38% say they use it multiple times an hour, and 16% report almost constant use.

So, we're spending a lot of time on social media! How do we use it? Mesai et al. (2015) say that there are five key behaviors that we use with social media.

1. We use it to broadcast information—or to share what's going on in our lives or world.
2. We use it to receive feedback on the information that we share. So, if we share about a trip we've taken, we'll also use social media to look for people's response to what we shared.
3. We observe what others have shared.
4. We share our own feedback on those things that others have broadcasted.
5. We compare ourselves to others. This is an important part of using social media to understand. We are not just sharing with and receiving information from others, we are actually looking at what others are sharing and comparing ourselves, our lives, our experiences, and perceived value with them.

It's also important to know that social media provides us with a consistent supply of social rewards. When our posts are liked, when we get new friend or connection requests, and positive responses to what we share, it activates our brain's reward system and shapes reinforcement learning, making us want to come back for more (Sherman et al. 2018). This is exactly how face-to-face social interactions act, and those who create social media platforms are looking for new ways to increase our interactions and provide more social rewards. This is why these platforms are so attractive to us, and why it is so difficult for some of us to ignore our social media for very long!

Social media has both positive and negative effects on all of us. So, it's important for parents to think about those for their children. How might using social media present challenges? It can interfere with developing emotional intelligence and developing face-to-face relationships. We learn to interact with one another and respond to things like facial expressions and body language. Spending more time on social media than in face-to-face interactions can make it difficult to learn how to respond to others effectively in face-to-face relationships.

Our use of social media might also distract from meaningful and important work. How many of us have planned to do something we thought was important, only to find ourselves sidetracked by scrolling through social media?

On the positive side, social media can increase our opportunities to learn new things. Also, it can lead to new relationships and build new skills when we join groups or follow accounts focused on our interests. As you're talking to your child about using social media effectively, keep in mind that social media is a tool, it is not good or bad in itself. You can work together to learn how to be proactive, using this tool with purpose.

Conversation starter

As noted above, social media can create meaningful connections with others and deepen relationships among friends or family who live far apart. However, it can also damage our interpersonal communication abilities, create feelings of inadequacy, waste huge amounts of time, and more! To begin a conversation about social media with your adolescent, start by checking in with them and asking which social media they use or would like to use and what they like/dislike about it. Visit with them about how friendships have been richer because of social media and then also what damage and harm they have seen social media cause in their own life.

Let's get started!

Create a social media collage

- ❍ Working alongside your child, each of you will write or type out your usernames for each social media platform you use.
- ❍ Copy and paste the following:
    - – Profile pictures of the past year or two
    - – Posts from the past weeks or months (level of social media activity will dictate how far back to go without the number of posts becoming excessive!)
    - – Recent selfies
    - – Information shared in "about" pages
    - – A few posts you have "liked" recently
    - – A few posts you have been tagged in by others
- ❍ Choose how you want to create a collage. You could cut out the various pictures and posts and glue them on a larger piece of paper. You could cut out the various pictures and posts and simply lay them out on a table to make a visual collage.

- Reflect together on what you see using the following questions:
  - How might others view you if this is all they see?
  - Does this match who you are in real life?
  - What does this say about how you view yourself and what you think is important?
  - Is this how you want others to see you?

Take it to the next level!

Challenge yourself with a digital detox! In theory, the idea of logging off all social media for a period of time sounds easy, but in reality, the addictive nature of social media and the algorithms in place to keep you scrolling make this a tough challenge! Decide on an amount of time and then designate the time you will stay completely off all social media. Make choices on how to make this work for you and your child! You might swap phones and change the password for the other person so they can't access their social media. Make sure to write down the new passwords somewhere so you can access your accounts later! You might choose to simply delete the apps for the chosen timeframe. Keep in mind you can always access each platform from a browser, so this might not be the most secure option.

At the end of the agreed upon detox time, discuss how it went. Think about how you each felt. What felt hard? What felt easy or maybe even freeing? What did you learn about yourself? What might you change going forward?

References

Broadband Search, Surprising Social Media Statistics (2021). https://www.broadbandsearch.net/blog/social-media-facts-statistics adapted from "Social Media Use in 2021." Pew Research Center, Washington, D.C. (April 7, 2021). https://www.pewresearch.org/internet/2021/04/07/social-media-use-in-2021/

Meshi, Tamir, and Heekeren, (2015). The emerging neuroscience of social media. *Trends in Cognitive Sciences,* 19(12), 771-782. DOI 10.1016/j.tics.2015.09.004

Rideout, V., and Robb, M. B. (2019). *The Common Sense census: Media use by tweens and teens, 2019.* San Francisco, CA: Common Sense Media.

Sherman, L.E., Hernandez, L.M., Greenfield, P.M., & Dapretto, M. (2018). What the brain 'Likes': neural correlates of providing feedback on social media. *Social Cognitive and Affective Neuroscience,* 699-707.

Pornography, Sexual Self Efficacy and Children

Question: How can parents prepare their child to deal with exposure to pornography while online?

Overview: In this section, parents will learn about the concept of sexual self-efficacy and gain knowledge about how to help children learn to respond to exposure when online.

What does the research say about Sexual Self Efficacy and Pornography?

When someone has sexual self-efficacy, she is able to see herself as a person who can make decisions about what happens to her sexually. He knows how to say yes and no to sexual behaviors and relationships. She knows how to ask for consent from a partner before engaging in sexual behaviors and how to demand that others ask for consent. When we're talking about sexual behaviors, we are not just talking about intercourse, but any kind of behavior linked to sexual attraction, including things like flirting, holding hands, and other verbal and physical interactions.

In order to help children thrive, parents need to connect with them through talking often and openly, build competence by providing kids with information about physical development and facts about sex and sexuality, and encourage confidence through helping kids think through specific scenarios that might cause difficulty and making a plan to handle them. Sexual self-efficacy grows in importance as children get older. Middle school is an important time to begin to build skills that your child will use later in life to help them use agency in making choices about their own sexual behaviors. Agency is viewing oneself as an active participant in one's own life, taking responsibility for one's decisions and feeling the power to act to achieve one's own goals and desires.

This is the time when you must start talking about pornography. For younger children, or those just entering middle school, a simple conversation might start with, "Sometimes when kids have questions about sex, they look online. But they may end up seeing things that they weren't planning to see." You can ask if they've ever heard of that or seen something that they weren't expecting. If they have seen pornography, allow them to talk about how they felt about it.

It's especially important to talk about the implications of viewing pornography. For example, many of the sexual acts depicted in pornography are not consistent with mutually respectful and satisfying sexual relationships. There are acts and behaviors that many individuals and couples are not interested in and that could cause harm. Pornography also often depicts women as sexual objects for the pleasure of men, pure objectification without a focus on the woman's pleasure. You need to talk with your child about the fact that in real life, people may not be interested in some of the acts that pornography portrays, and that in a healthy sexual relationship, a partner must always be able to say no and to make their own decisions about what they want to engage in.

Watching pornography can give children an unrealistic idea of what is involved in healthy sexual relationships. It can also give them an unrealistic idea of what bodies should look like, and for young men can cause sexual dysfunction where they are only aroused by media, but not by a real person with whom they are in a relationship.

For middle schoolers, an introduction to this conversation will open doors for future, more specific conversations as your child gets older. However, if you believe that your early adolescent is heavily involved with pornography, you will need to get into details as soon as possible. The truth is, pornography can distort a child's understanding of healthy sexual relationships and behaviors, so it's vital that adults do not shy away from these conversations.

It's important that parents start thinking about how to address issues of sexuality early on so that you can provide your child with the best information possible.

The key thing to remember regarding talking about sex is that you want to allow the conversation to flow naturally. When I ask college students what they would tell parents about talking with children about sex, they always say that in their own experience, it's more comfortable when parents talk about sex in small, natural increments rather than having one big "talk." In fact, many of the college students said that when their parents took the "sex talk" approach, they felt awkward. They wished that their parents had taken more opportunities to address issues as they arose rather than having a formal talk.

Conversation starter

Sexualized media often depicts sexuality void of context. A good starting point is to talk about how we share physical affection with those who we care about. We share hugs as a family because we love each other. People hold hands, kiss, hug and share other physical affection as a way of expressing their care. This begins to help kids see physical affection in the context of relationships.

When you're ready to talk with your child about sexual intercourse, you can talk about it as an extension of physical affection that two people share who care about each other. It's not scary; it's a beautiful and natural way of sharing affection in a committed relationship.

Sexualized media depicts female sexuality as an object for someone else's pleasure. You want to build your child's understanding of both male and female sexuality as mutual. Talk to them about how people share physical affection with one another because they want to, not because it's expected.

When your child asks you a question or shares something that was said to them by a peer or seen on a media source, listen and answer them honestly. You want your child to see you as their first source of information about sex and sexuality.

Don't shame your child for asking questions or expressing sexual desires. You want them to know that they can come to you to talk about sex. As your child gets older and becomes involved in romantic relationships, you want to have set the stage for them to feel free to talk with you. Research tells us that those adolescents who feel that there is open communication with their parents about sexuality engage in less risky sexual behaviors.

Talk to your kids about pornography as young as 9 or 10. I know this sounds very early, but especially if your child has free access to the Internet, you must address this early. Many boys who struggle with pornography addiction start looking at Internet pornography as young as 11. Addiction to Internet pornography can cause serious problems for a child in learning to build real life relationships.

These are just a few ideas to keep in mind as you think about talking with your kids about sex. The main point is to see sexuality as a normal, natural part of life and development. Your child is a little person with an emerging sense of sexuality. Don't be afraid of that, instead, approach those feelings and thoughts just like you do with anything else that they're learning. When you think of it that way, it helps you take advantage of natural opportunities for conversation and sharing of information with your child.

Let's Get Started!

This topic differs from others in this book because of the highly sensitive nature and even questions of legality. Obviously, this topic will be more conversation focused.

After engaging in some of the conversation above, discuss in more detail how your child might find themselves on an unexpected pornographic site or with some sort of popup that contains pornographic images or video. Depending on the age and maturity of your child, use any of the following conversation ideas to help their understanding.

1. "As we have discussed, many producers of pornography take normal, intimate, and good behaviors and distort them in some way. They often distort body parts by using special digital effects or emphasizing them in potentially unhealthy ways. Let's imagine you are working on a project about the human body for school and you need to search information about a body system. The search might take you to a link or site that does not contain scientific information about the body, but rather, exploitive information." Then discuss how to avoid this happening and how to handle it if it does happen.

2. "There are words that mean more than one thing! A simple example is the word 'bat.' A bat can mean either a baseball bat or a bat that is an animal. Can you think of any others? There are some words that are spelled the same way, but one meaning is common and the other is slang or sexual in nature. One example of this might be the word 'ball.' What do you

think might happen if you are interested in various kinds of balls used in a particular sport and just searched the internet for 'balls?'" Follow your child's lead on how to continue this conversation. (The authors of this book apologize for the need to include such crass examples!)

3. With the huge increase in the use of videoconferencing platforms like Zoom, there is always a risk of someone accessing the videoconference seeking to do harm. I (Amy) was on a Zoom webinar with an author introducing his new book when the call got "Zoom-bombed" by someone using horrific racial slurs and embedding pornographic video across the screen. Needless to say, the hosts immediately ended the call, but the experience was traumatic and disturbing. Most videoconferences now include passwords or logins, but there is always that possibility of a nefarious intrusion. Discuss with your child how to stay as safe as possible using videoconferencing platforms.

Take it to the next level!

Your child's exposure to pornography is a matter of "when," not "if." Knowing that it is so pervasive and there are many ways to accidentally and intentionally access pornography, it is important to normalize stumbling upon pornography and lowering the temperature about your child alerting you to seeing something that they should not have seen. With this in mind, make a plan for when they encounter pornography that suits your child. The following idea is simply one of several possibilities, so think about your own child and decide what will feel the least awkward and the most empowering for that individual child. For example, one idea is creating tangible, easy steps. If something potentially pornographic pops up on their screen or if they click to something inappropriate, employ the following plan:

1. Immediately click the "back" button. This will take the image or video off the screen and allow the child to seek your assistance.

2. Get up right that moment and come find a parent or guardian to help check out the situation further.

3. Look into whatever the child was exposed to and check in with them without any shaming language or tone.

Media Creation

Question: How can parents help children learn to see themselves as media creators who can effectively share their own perspective with others?

Overview: In this final section, children will have the opportunity to synthesize all the components of media consumption they have learned throughout these workbook activities.

What does the research say about media creation?

Having seen themselves as media critics, children can also learn to think of themselves as media makers. Parents can help their child move from someone who passively accepts images and narratives presented by the media to someone who actively creates their own view, and then works to influence the views of those around them. Using high quality cameras on their laptop or smartphone, many children can easily record video and audio. Most adolescents are familiar with YouTube, TikTok, and other sharing sites and can use those to share their creations widely. Large media corporations are no longer the only ones who can widely disseminate their viewpoint. Now, children are capable of crafting their own stories and sharing their own worldviews widely. As they work to develop their ideas and express their values and belief systems, children will become even more aware of the techniques that media makers use to connect with and persuade their audience.

Media is influential. The beauty of artistic expression through various forms of media is that it can touch the audience right where they are. Young content creators can learn to construct media messages from a perspective of social responsibility. Content creators work with mediums that move their audience, that persuade them, that make them believe, that make them laugh or cry. Media is a beautiful and powerful force. Children can learn to believe in the beauty that they can create and to think of the influence that they can wield through being message creators.

Using simple techniques and accessible tools, children can make potent statements promoting their own value systems. This provides an opportunity for positive influence as the content creator is adding something to popular conversation. Rather than sitting back and being an armchair critic who feels powerless, beginning to think and act like a maker will give children the tools to view themselves as someone who has something important to share.

The key is that we have the tools to create online content that we want to see and to comment critically and publicly upon products and programming that we do not like. Children can use these ideas to make a public statement promoting their own values or questioning those promoted by particular programs or products. If a child is really interested in producing quality media content, they can try to get it produced professionally. Help them look for workshops, contests, and other opportunities to share the work as a media maker.

Conversation starter

Many children and teens experiment with creating videos and other media content for fun. Obviously, others post created content on social media platforms. Media creation is such a common part of our cultural narrative, most people do not consider themselves media creators, they just post with regularity just like eating lunch or taking a shower. Helping reframe posting on social media as media creation awakens tweens and teens to the intentionality that should accompany posting online.

Let's get started!

- ❍ In this activity, you and your child will practice being thoughtful content creators.
- ❍ Before diving in, take a little time to provide a quick primer on the rhetorical proofs of ethos, pathos, and logos.
- ❍ The basic definitions are:
  - Ethos: credibility, how credible the audience/reader perceives the writer or speaker to be
  - Pathos: emotional connection, how are feelings engaged
  - Logos: facts, logic
- ❍ The task is to create a persuasive post of your choice using ethos, pathos, and/or logos and considering the topics covered in this workbook.
  - Determining the target audience
  - Intent of the message
  - Online vs. in-person identity
  - Perspectives a media message takes
  - Considerations of bias
  - Portrayal of stereotypes
  - The permanence of online content
  - Recognizing fake news
  - The sway of celebrity

Take it to the next level!

It's time to create a family media checklist! The purpose of this final activity is to develop a checklist each member of the family could use to think more purposefully about the media they are consuming. Ask children to consider each of the topics or ideas one might consider when consuming media. Be sure to think about the various topics in this book (list is in the previous section).

Checklists give structure to observation beyond just thinking about something. They are tangible and provide a sense of accountability. Think through what criteria might be for evaluating a media message.

Examples of potential checklist items:

- ❍ The target audience of this media is ________________.
- ❍ A harmful stereotype I noticed is ________________.

Once the checklist is created and approved by all family members, place a copy of the checklist in all areas of the home where someone might be consuming media.

Conclusion

As we think back to Bronfenbrenner's model, we are reminded that you are part of your child's microsystem which is the closest interaction to an individual. Media, as part of the exosystem, and culture, part of the macrosystem, certainly interact with your child, but from more of a distance. In the **process** of interacting with your child and who they are as a **person** at this moment in **time,** you can lead and guide them as they navigate the **context** that shapes their understanding of and ability to respond to media.

As parents ourselves, we firmly believe that you are one of the most powerful influences on your child's development and their ability to be effective consumers and creators of media. We hope the content of this book has left you feeling empowered and more capable to navigate important conversations and decisions about media with your child and on your way to teaching your child how to be a more purposeful media creator and consumer!

About the Authors

Amy Boone, M.Ed. is a Texas certified teacher and has taught students from pre-kindergarten to graduate school. She is the Teaching and Learning Specialist for the Adams Center for Teaching and Learning at Abilene Christian University. She has written about positive media production and piloted many of these lessons with gifted students in a summer gifted program. She is the co-author of the book *Creating and Consuming Media Messages with Purpose: A Guide for Educators*

Jennifer W. Shewmaker, Ph.D., is a nationally certified school psychologist who has worked with thousands of families, children, and teachers in her career. She serves as the Provost at Lipscomb University, is the co-author of the books *Creating and Consuming Media Messages with Purpose: A Guide for Educators*, and author of *Sexualized Media Messages and Our Children.*

Printed in the USA
CPSIA information can be obtained
at www.ICGtesting.com
JSHW010150030724
65731JS00006B/20

9 781953 360243